I0603640

HILLSBORO PUBLIC LIBRARIES
Hillsboro, OR
Member of Washington County
COOPERATIVE LIBRARY SERVICES

21st Century Skills Library

REAL WORLD MATH: PERSONAL FINANCE

WHAT IS MONEY?

Cecilia Minden

Cherry Lake Publishing
Ann Arbor, Michigan

HILLSBORO PUBLIC LIBRARIES
Hillsboro, OR
Member of Washington County
COOPERATIVE LIBRARY SERVICES

Published in the United States of America by Cherry Lake Publishing
Ann Arbor, Michigan
www.cherrylakepublishing.com

Math Education Adviser: Tonya Walker, MA, Boston University

Finance Adviser: Jill Klooster, CPA, Kitchenmaster & Company

Photo Credits: Cover and page 1, ©Lim Yong Hian, used under license from
Shutterstock, Inc.; page 4, ©Taolmor, used under license from Shutterstock, Inc.;
page 7, ©North Wind Picture Archives/Alamy; page 8, ©Les Byerley, used under
license from Shutterstock, Inc.; page 11, ©Arlene Jean Gee, used under license
from Shutterstock, Inc.; page 13, ©Joseph, used under license from Shutterstock, Inc.;
page 14, ©Ilene MacDonald/Alamy; page 16, ©iStockphoto.com/Yuri_Arcurs; page 18,
©iStockphoto.com/echo1; page 21, ©Ian Shaw/Alamy; page 24, ©afotoshop, used under
license from Shutterstock, Inc.; page 26, ©Monkey Business Images, used under license
from Shutterstock, Inc.

Copyright ©2009 by Cherry Lake Publishing
All rights reserved. No part of this book may be reproduced or utilized in any
form or by any means without written permission from the publisher.

Library of Congress Cataloging-in-Publication Data
Minden, Cecilia.
What Is Money?/ by Cecilia Minden.
  p. cm.—(Real world math)
Includes index.
ISBN-13: 978-1-60279-312-5
ISBN-10: 1-60279-312-3
1. Money—Juvenile literature. I. Title.
HG221.5.M56 2009
332.4—dc22   2008025514

4054 1327 06/09

Cherry Lake Publishing would like to acknowledge the work of
The Partnership for 21st Century Skills.
Please visit www.21stcenturyskills.org for more information.

TABLE OF CONTENTS

CHAPTER ONE

ROCKS, CORN, AND SALT

Roman coins featured important rulers or events. Ancient coins provide information for experts who study the past.

Have you ever received money as a gift? Maybe it was in the form of a

gift card for on online retailer such as Apple iTunes. Did you know that

if you lived thousands of years ago, the "money" you received might have

been rocks or shells?

In ancient times, people exchanged goods for other goods or services. For example, a bushel of corn might be traded for a bushel of potatoes. This is called **bartering**. But bartering can become complicated. After all, how many bushels of wheat should be traded for a cow?

People began using **currency**. Currency puts a value on a product. Another name for currency is money. It wasn't always the kind of money we use today. Salt, for example, was very valuable because it helped to preserve food. Blocks of salt were sometimes used as currency. Barley, beads, and feathers have all been used as currency in the past.

Some people think that the first coins came from the ancient kingdom of Lydia. Today, we know Lydia as the country of Turkey. Other people believe that the very first coins were bronze coins made in China thousands of years ago.

Learning & Innovation Skills

Over time, many countries created coins. Each country wanted its coins to look different from those of other countries. Designers acted on creative ideas and came up with unique "looks" for their coins. Coins were made of metals of different values, such as gold, silver, copper, and bronze. Some were round. Others were square. Chinese coins were round with a square hole in the middle! Artists designed coins that featured images of symbols, animals, and important rulers.

Why do you think it was important that coins from different countries have their own original or special designs?

The Chinese came up with another way to make buying and selling easier. They started using paper to represent money. The government printed pieces of paper called receipts. Special designs were used so no one could copy the paper. Each receipt had a fixed value. One advantage of paper money is that it is much lighter than coins.

Early European settlers in what is now the United States brought coins from many different countries. They often bartered with crops such as corn and tobacco. They also traded with Native Americans. Native American money was made of shells. The shells were woven into belts and bracelets and called wampum.

Fur was a popular item with European traders. Native Americans traded animal pelts for guns, tools, and other European products.

The British government did not allow the colonists to print their own money. They had to use a combination of coins, wampum, and goods to buy and sell products.

After the colonists declared their independence, they created money for the new United States. How was the U.S. money system developed? Who creates all the money?

Sharpen your pencils, get a fresh pad of paper, and keep a calculator handy. We'll use our math skills to answer those questions and learn more about money.

CHAPTER TWO

MAKING MONEY

The U.S. Mint in Philadelphia, Pennsylvania, was the first mint established in the United States. It has operated in four different locations in the city.

One of the first acts of the Continental Congress was to establish a currency system for the new country. The first U.S. Mint was created in Philadelphia, Pennsylvania, in 1782. A mint is where coins are made.

In 2006, 15.5 billion coins were produced in the United States. Today, circulating coins are minted in Philadelphia and in Denver, Colorado. Coins from Denver are marked with a *D*. Coins from Philadelphia are marked with a *P*.

Certain words must appear on circulating coins. *Liberty, In God We Trust, United States of America,* and *E Pluribus Unum* (Latin for "out of many, one") appear on each U.S. coin. Each coin also has the denomination and year it was minted.

REAL WORLD MATH CHALLENGE

You've probably heard the expression a "ton of money." A ton of pennies is worth $3,630. A ton of quarters is worth $40,000. A ton of $1 bills amounts to $908,000.

How many pennies are there in a ton? How many quarters are in a ton? How many more $1 bills should be added to a ton to make it total $1 million?

(Turn to page 29 for the answers)

21st Century Content

In 2003, the U.S. Mint launched a new program. It was called the Artist Infusion Program. One of their tasks would be to help design the 50 state quarters. Several hundred artists applied, and 24 were selected. They were master designers, professional artists, and students enrolled in visual arts programs. Each year, different artists are added as others leave the program.

Artists sometimes have trouble finding employment opportunities. This program is one innovative way of creating new career options for artists. Who designed your state's quarter?

A coin begins with an artist's design that has been approved by the U.S. Congress. Then a plastic model of the coin is created. A machine copies the design from the plastic coin onto a small metal die. A die is a device used for shaping objects. In a separate machine, sheets of metal are cut into disks. These disks, called blanks, are heated, cooled, cleaned, and shaped. The dies are put inside a machine called a coin press. A coin is minted when this machine presses the dies into the blanks. Each press creates 750 new coins a minute! The coins are bagged, weighed, and safely stored until distributed.

In 1861, the U.S. Treasury began printing paper money. Today, paper currency in the United States

Canadian loonies get their name from the bird—the loon—that is pictured on the coin.

includes denominations of $1, $2, $5, $10, $20, $50, and $100.

The Department of Engraving and Printing is responsible for printing

all U.S. paper currency. Money is printed in Washington, DC, and

Fort Worth, Texas.

Each country's paper money looks different. Canadian money, for example, features many colors and images. Canadians don't have paper bills for their $1 or $2 denominations. Instead, they use a $1 coin called a loonie. The $2 coin is called a toonie. The Royal Canadian Mint produces all circulating coins in Canada as well as certain coins for other countries.

The paper for U.S. currency is made up of a special blend of cotton and linen. Red and blue fibers are included in the blend. Currency is made to stand up to a lot of use. Even so, the average life of a $5 bill is approximately 16 months.

Paper money is more easily copied than coins. Dishonest people try to create counterfeit money. It looks like the real thing, but it has no value. If you look at a bill very carefully, you will see the many safeguards that indicate it is real money. The U.S. Treasury makes changes on

*Why do you think that the exact formula for the ink
used to print U.S. currency is kept secret?*

the bills every 7 to 10 years. These changes make it more difficult to copy

U.S. currency.

The United States uses **intaglio printing** to give bills a one-of-a-kind

look. Intaglio printing involves very fine line engraving to create images

and designs on the bills.

Serial numbers are one way to keep track of paper money and help detect counterfeiting.

Security threads are also used on some denominations. They make it more difficult to copy the paper with a color copier. They also help prevent counterfeiters from changing one bill to another. For example, they keep someone from changing a $10 bill into a $100 bill.

Each bill also has a serial number and Treasury seal. No two serial numbers are the same.

In March 2008, a new $5 bill was issued using the latest security techniques. Hold a new $5 bill up to the light to see if you can spot the watermarks. Look for three small 5s and one large 5. Did you find the security thread? Look for the letters *USA* and the number 5 along the thread line. The $5 bill accounts for 9 percent of all bills in circulation. The U.S. Treasury wanted to make sure it was very difficult to copy!

Now you know about the history of money and how it is produced. Let's explore how math can help us understand why those pieces of metal and paper are so valuable.

CHAPTER THREE

DO THE MATH: WHY MONEY HAS VALUE

U.S. coins and currency can be used to buy things in stores throughout the United States.

What if a neighbor hired you to build a fence but offered to pay you with a box of shells from the beach instead of cash? You would be upset because the shells have no value at a store. Money is valuable because you can use it to get the goods and services you need or want.

When you shop, the stores accept your money because they can use it to purchase more things for their businesses. The stores also use it to pay employees. The workers use the money they earn to buy things from other stores. They also deposit money in the bank for future purchases. Producing, consuming, and distributing goods are all part of our economic system.

Banks manage their accounts, but who is managing all the banks? In 1913, Congress created the Federal Reserve System when President Woodrow Wilson signed the Federal Reserve Act. The Federal Reserve System is also known as the Fed. The purpose of the Fed is to provide a stable monetary system for U.S. money. Think of it as a bank for the other banks. It is also the bank for our government. One of the most important jobs of the Fed is keeping prices stable and interest rates low.

Some day you may take out a loan called a mortgage to purchase a home.
You may be able to negotiate interest rates with the mortgage lender.

Interest rates are what you pay when you borrow money. If interest rates

are low, borrowers can pay off debts and pay only a small amount of

interest money. When interest rates are high, borrowers end up paying a

lot of interest money.

REAL WORLD MATH CHALLENGE

Joseph borrowed $60 from his brother Mike. They agreed that Joseph would pay Mike $20 a week plus 3 percent interest on the balance of the loan until it is paid off. **How long will it take Joseph to pay off his loan? How much interest will Joseph pay Mike each week? How much total interest will Joseph pay on this loan? Remember to calculate interest before subtracting each week's payment.**

(Turn to page 29 for the answers)

Money always has some value, but the actual value of the dollar changes.

The changes are caused by inflation and deflation. Inflation happens

when the demand for an item goes up but the supply goes down. Think of

a box of 100 baseballs. Each one can be traded for a $1 bill. One summer,

everyone wants to buy those baseballs. There aren't enough baseballs for

everyone who wants one. So some people are willing to pay $100 for a

baseball. The baseball hasn't changed. It is still the same $1 product, but the

21st Century Content

Money doesn't last forever. What happens to currency when it is too damaged to use? It loses its value. The U.S. Treasury will redeem, or buy back, money that is badly damaged. It is a free service to the public. One-dollar bills are some of the most common bills replaced. Experts in the Office of Currency Standards must approve the reimbursement of the money. It can be redeemed only for the exact value of the bill.

Staying informed about government services like this one is important. It can mean the difference between simply throwing away damaged money and taking the steps to get replacement cash!

demand has caused the price to rise. This is inflation. The next summer, there is no demand for baseballs so they decrease in value. This is deflation. Inflation and deflation are very important in determining the value of money in our economy.

The Bank of Canada in Ottawa, Ontario, is in charge of many financial policies and services in Canada. It is also the bank for the government. An important goal of the institution is to keep the value of Canadian currency high by keeping inflation low.

You know about coins and paper money. You know about the value of money. Next we'll explore different kinds of money.

CHAPTER FOUR

DO THE MATH: DIFFERENT KINDS OF MONEY

Gold is a precious metal that has been used as money for centuries.

When banks first began using paper notes or bills, the money

represented actual gold or silver. Anyone could go to a bank in the United

States and trade paper money for gold or silver. It was called the gold standard. In the 1970s, President Richard Nixon ended the gold

standard in the United States. Our money today is called **fiat money**.

The currency we use is determined to be legal trade by our government.

A paper bill itself has no value. The value of the money comes from

supply and demand.

Another kind of money is credit money. When you use credit money,

you purchase a product but promise to pay for it in the future. Banks issue

loans, but you also have to pay interest. Short-term loans, such as credit

card purchases, have higher rates. Long-term loans used to pay for things

such as homes or cars have lower interest rates. The rates are lower because

you pay the loan back over a longer period of time.

You can also buy and sell with checks and electronic transfers. Your

friend Luke sells you his old skateboard. You write Luke a check. A check

REAL WORLD MATH CHALLENGE

Gift cards are another type of currency. When you receive a gift card, someone has already paid the amount on the gift card for you. Apple, Inc. sells gift cards that you can use online to purchase music for your MP3 player. Julie received a $25 Apple iTunes gift card from her grandmother for her birthday. Each song purchased online costs $0.99. Julie has already bought 17 songs with her gift card. Now she wants to buy her favorite band's new album. The album costs $9.99. **How much of the gift card money has Julie already spent? Does she have enough money left on the iTunes card to pay for the new album? If not, how much more money will she need to buy the album?**

(Turn to page 29 for the answers)

is a written promise from you that a business or person will receive money in the amount that the check states. Luke deposits it in his bank account.

Your bank deducts the amount from your account and sends it to Luke's bank, where it is deposited in his account. This is called an electronic money transfer. No actual money was used.

Euro notes are colorful. Different denominations feature different colors.

We've learned about money in the United States, but foreign currency

plays a big part in our nation's economy. We live in a global economy.

The value of currency in one country has an impact on the value of

currency in another country. The value of money from one country in a different country is called the exchange rate. At one point in 2008, $1.00 of American currency equaled approximately C$1.00313 of Canadian currency. This means that American money had a slightly lower value than Canadian money. The rate varies from country to country and changes frequently.

We've explored many different kinds of money in the United States and overseas. Let's use our math skills to see how all of this can help you manage your money.

In the late 1990s, the governments of several European countries decided to work together for a more stable economy. Showing initiative and leadership, they agreed to use the same currency—the Euro. Instead of each nation having its own money, all the nations could now use one kind of money throughout the region. Achieving this outcome took flexibility and cooperation on the part of each country. Representatives from different nations had to work together through complex issues and reach a common goal. The Euro is legal currency in participating countries such as Italy, Spain, Portugal, and France.

What are some advantages of having several countries share a common currency?

CHAPTER FIVE

MAKE YOUR MONEY COUNT FOR YOU!

Compare prices when you go shopping. It's a smart habit that can help you save money on purchases.

You may think the money you spend doesn't make a difference in the economic system. Think again. There are millions of kids your age in the United States. Many of them spend hundreds of dollars of their own money each year. That adds up to millions of dollars going into our economy. Making good shopping choices not only helps you, it helps the economy, too.

It is important to start practicing good math and money management skills now. They will give you the tools you need to have a better financial future.

The best place to begin is with a plan. A plan to keep track of your money is called a budget. A budget should include your assets (income) and expenditures (expenses). Begin by keeping a journal of your expenses for a few weeks. Write down everything. Keeping track of your money helps you see what your greatest expenditures are.

Learn to tell the difference between wants and needs. Before you make a purchase, stop and ask yourself if you need this or would just like to have this.

You can also use the money you have to make more money. Banks will pay you interest on the money you keep in a savings account. You can also earn interest on other investments. To figure out how fast you can double your money, use the "Rule of 72." Simply take 72, and divide it by the interest rate. The answer is the number of years it will take to double the original amount of money.

"Money" has evolved in many ways over the course of history. Salt and shells have been replaced by electronic transfers and credit cards. What hasn't changed is the practice of exchanging something of value for something you want or need.

How are you spending or saving your money today?

REAL WORLD MATH CHALLENGE

Mrs. Garcia is keeping track of expenses. She notices that the price of milk is increasing. Over 4 months, she paid $2.45, $2.60, $2.75, and $2.90. **What is the difference between the first and second months' milk prices? Based on the listed prices, what do you predict the cost will be next month? How much will milk increase over this 5-month period?**

(Turn to page 29 for the answers)

REAL WORLD MATH CHALLENGE ANSWERS

Chapter Two
Page 12

There are 363,000 pennies in a ton.

$3,630 \div .01 = 363,000$

There are 160,000 quarters in a ton.

$40,000 \div .25 = 160,000$

You need $92,000 more $1 bills to equal $1 million.

$\$1,000,000 - \$908,000 = \$92,000$

Chapter Three
Page 19

Joseph will pay off the loan in 3 weeks.

$\$60 \div \$20 = 3$ weeks

He will pay Mike $1.80 in interest the first week.

$\$60 \times 0.03 = \$1.80$

After the first week, Joseph's balance is $40.

$\$60 - \$20 = \$40$

He will pay Mike $1.20 in interest the second week.

$\$40 \times 0.03 = \$1.20$

After the second week, Joseph's balance is $20.

$\$40 - \$20 = \$20$

He will pay Mike $0.60 in interest the final week.

$\$20 \times 0.03 = \$0.60$

After the final week, Joseph's balance is $0.

$\$20 - \$20 = \$0$

Joseph paid Mike $3.60 in total interest.

$\$1.80 + \$1.20 + \$0.60 = \$3.60$

Chapter Four
Page 23

Julie has already spent $16.83.

17 songs x $0.99 = $16.83

She has $8.17 remaining on the iTunes gift card.

$\$25 - \$16.83 = \$8.17$

She will need an additional $1.82 to purchase the album.

$\$9.99 - \$8.17 = \$1.82$

Chapter Five
Page 28

The milk increased by $0.15 from the first to the second month.

$\$2.60 - \$2.45 = \$0.15$

Based on the previous prices, the milk will cost $3.05 next month.

$\$2.90 + \$0.15 = \$3.05$

Milk will have increased by $0.60 over 5 months.

$\$3.05 - \$2.45 = \$0.60$

GLOSSARY

bartering (BAR-tur-eeng) trading products, goods, or services instead of using money

circulating (SUR-kyoo-late-ing) passing something, such as coins or currency, from person to person

counterfeit (KOUN-tur-fit) made to look like something else in order to deceive

currency (KUR-uhn-see) money in circulation that is used in a particular country

deflation (di-FLAY-shuhn) a general price decrease for goods and services

denomination (di-nom-uh-NAY-shuhn) the value of a single bill or coin

economic system (ek-uh-NOM-ik SISS-tuhm) the production, distribution, and consumption of goods and services

fiat money (FEE-it MUH-nee) paper currency that cannot be exchanged for gold or silver

inflation (in-FLAY-shuhn) a general price increase for goods and services

intaglio printing (in-TAH-lee-o PRIN-teeng) a printing process used to make paper currency that involves a special type of engraving

monetary (MON-uh-tair-ee) relating to money

serial number (SIHR-ee-uhl NUM-bur) a unique number given to each bill of currency to help prevent counterfeiting

watermarks (WAH-tur-markss) marks or designs on paper currency that are visible only when the paper is held up to a light source

FOR MORE INFORMATION

Books

Cribb, Joe. *Money.* New York: DK Publishing, 2005.

Harman, Hollis Page. *Money Sense for Kids!* Hauppauge, NY: Barron's, 2004.

Somervill, Barbara A. *The History of Money.* Chanhassen, MN: The Child's World, 2006.

Web Sites

Bank of Canada—Banque du Canada
www.bank-banque-canada.ca/
For more information about Canadian money

The Official Kids' Portal for the U.S. Government
www.kids.gov/k_5/k_5_money.shtml
Learn more about the money-making process and counterfeit currency

U.S. Department of the Treasury: For Kids
www.ustreas.gov/kids/
Explore the story behind the designs of different coins, or design your own money

Index

About the Author

Cecilia Minden, PhD, is a former classroom teacher and university professor. She now enjoys working as a literacy consultant and writer for school and library publications. She has written more than 50 books for children. Cecilia lives with her family near Chapel Hill, North Carolina.